# Would What would you be...?

## Questions to Find Out WHO and WHAT You Really Are

Justin Heimberg  &  David Gomberg

Published by Falls Media
565 Park Avenue, Suite 11E
New York, NY 10021

First Printing, November 2007
10 9 8 7 6 5 4 3 2
© Copyright Justin Heimberg and David Gomberg, 2007
All Rights Reserved


Design by Tom Schirtz


ISBN-13 978-0-9788178-5-5

# How To Use This Book

How not to use this book is more like it! There are countless uses. This thing is like the Silly Putty of books. It even bounces. Go ahead, try it!

Okay, so maybe the book doesn't bounce, but there really are all sorts of games to play with the questions in the book. All of the games and questions will help you learn about new or old friends and reveal how your friends see you and the rest of the world. Of course, you'll have to get through the laughter first! (If you can't, you may have a serious condition and should consult medical help immediately.)

You'll figure out some games on your own, but here are four fun ones:

### Game 1: *I Am Thinking of Someone We All Know.*
This is a way to use the book as a group game. One player thinks of someone who everybody in the group knows: a friend, a coworker, an enemy, a teacher, etc. This is the "name on the table." Other players take turns reading a randomly selected page of questions from the book. The player who is thinking of someone answers each question as if he were that person. After every page, have a player guess who you are thinking of.

Optional: If you want, you can all write down a bunch of people you know on scraps of paper, turn them over, and have the answerer pull a name from the pile.

## Game 2: *Conversation.*

Pretty simple. Read a question and answer it as yourself. If there is a group of you, everybody should answer the question. Suggest your own answers for what you think others are and discuss why. See who agrees and who disagrees. Debate. Deliberate. Arm-wrestle. Think about other people you know (your friends, family, bosses, etc.) and what they would be. When the conversation fades into silence and awkward stares— you guessed it—it's time to move on to the next question.

## Game 3: *Celebrity.*

Go back a page. Reread the directions for Game 1, but substitute "celebrity" for "someone who everybody in the group knows."

## Game 4: *Ninja Strike.*

Find a horde of bandits marauding caravans. Train in the martial arts, specializing in book warfare. Fashion this book into a throwing star or other deadly piece of weaponry. Defeat marauders.

# When Answering Questions...

As you answer questions, use your gut. Give answers that capture the essence of a person, both physically and in terms of one's personality.

If the question is, "If you were a weather forecast", and you or the person you are thinking of is volatile, with a temper, and generally angry, you might say "Cloudy with a chance of thunderstorms."

If the question asks, "If you were an animal", and you or the person you are thinking of is sly, sneaky, kind of roguish, you might say "a fox."

When answering, capture the core essence of a person rather than giving an answer based on associations. Let's say the question asked, "If you were a state, what state would you be?" You consider yourself (or the person you are thinking of) to be big in size and personality: loud, passionate, and fiery. You (or the person you are thinking of) are also, however, from Maine. But given the traits, Texas is a much better answer. Just because someone is from Maine, does not mean they would "be Maine."

Maine is a bad answer because it does not capture the essence of the person; it is just an association. Of course, there are no "wrong" answers, but there are inferior ones that bring shame upon you and your family. ☺

You can elaborate when you answer questions too. Let's say the question asks you: "If you were a soda, what would you be?" You might answer, "Diet Coke. Because I leave a bad aftertaste. And I seem sweet, but it's fake."

You can also say someone is part something and part something else. For example, if the question is "If you were a type of footwear, what would you be," you might answer "Mainly a high heel, but at times a flip-flop." Or if asked what cable channel you are, you could say, "I used to be MTV, was briefly VH1, and now I am CNN."

### Passing
If you feel you don't have a good answer, and giving one will throw people off, pass, and move onto the next question. Dude, it all makes us stronger in the end.

*Questions of Character:*
Occasionally you will get a question that veers from the general format. Christ, why would we do that?! Because these questions will also give you a sense of what you or the person you are thinking of is all about. These questions will be labeled "Question of character." Answer them as you would answer the normal questions.

If you were a **color**, what would you be?

If you were a **dog**, what breed would you be? What would your bark sound like?

If you were a *Simpsons* **character**, who would you be?

If you were a **type of car**, what make and model would you be? What condition are you in? How many miles do you have on you?

**YOU MUST CHOOSE!**

**If you were a punctuation mark**, what would you be?
A few to choose from: ? ! ; * , / ( ) $ & . and don't forget the
versatile #, the smug ∧ , or the wily ~

**If you were a beat**, what would you be? (Drum it or beatbox it.)

**If you were a type of cheese**, what would you be?

**If you were a member of the *A-Team***, which character
would you be?

Things to consider: Are you crazy? Are you slick and good-looking? Do you enjoy the
culmination of a plan? Are you a large black man with a Mohawk who wears a preposterous
amount of jewelry and has an aversion to air travel?

**YOU MUST CHOOSE!**

**If you were a weather forecast**, what would you be? Give the forecast as if a weatherman: For example, "Mostly sunny with a chance of afternoon thunderstorms. Some storms might be severe, becoming cooler at night..."

**If you were a state**, which would you be?

Things to consider: Are you dry? Hot? Do you have a panhandle?

**If you were a Beatle**, which one would you be?

**If you were a tattoo**, what would you be and on what part of the body?

*Chinese symbol for "need for attention."*

**YOU MUST CHOOSE!**

3

# Physical Phun!

**If you were a facial expression**, what would you be? (Make it.)

**If you were a walk** (a strut, a trot, an affected limp for sympathy, etc.), what would you be? (Walk it.)

**If you were a sexual position**, what would you be? (Demonstrate it with five thrusts. Use another person if need be.)

*Question of character:*

**If you had to partake in sexual role-playing, what fantasy** would appeal to you most: a) "Teacher Keeps Bookish Student after Class"; b) "Football Player Meets Cheerleader in Locker Room"; or c) "Post-Roast Beef Sandwich Consumption Run-in with Anonymous Thin Moroccan in Arby's Bathroom Stall"?

**YOU MUST CHOOSE!**

If you were a **font**, which would you be?

META - BOLD CAPS

**Serpentine**   *Yikes*

**Tiki Sands**   **RUBBER STAMP**

*Balzano*   **ATCMapleUltra**   *Jokerman*

Big Caslon   Interstate Hairline

*Nuptial Script*

⊕ⵣ■ℽ⌂ⵣ■ℽ◆

Arial   *Cat Krap*   **Spumoni**

Did you know? The font that gets laid the most is
*French Script*, while **Goudy Stout** is gay. Bauhaus
and Lucida Sans Unicode are both virgins.

**YOU MUST CHOOSE!**

If you were a **finger**, which would you be (Pinky, Ring, Middle, Index, Thumb)?

If you were a **movie genre**, what would you be? What would your Motion Picture Association movie rating be? (G, PG, R, etc.)

If you were a **city**, which would you be?

Things to consider: Are you fast-paced? Laid-back? Do you have a giant arch protruding from you?

If you were a **painting**, what would you be? If you can't think of any, choose between *The Starry Night* by Vincent Van Gogh, a calm landscape scene of an ocean with a lighthouse, a wild and abstract Jackson Pollock splatter-painting, and *Dogs Playing Poker*.

**YOU MUST CHOOSE!**

For the following questions, use your cell phones or PDAs to answer.

**If you were a cell phone ring**, what would you be? Go through your phone's rings until you get the best one.

**If you were a type of cell phone or PDA** (iPhone, Blackberry, etc.), what would you be? What if you were a PDA as in public display of affection? (Demonstrate it.)

**If you were a text message using only 5 letters**, what would you be? (Text it.)

*Question of character:*

Who would be your **ideal phone sex partner?**
Some ideas: Angelina Jolie, Russell Crowe, Jenna Jameson, Lou Dobbs, Marcel Marceau, the *Inside the NFL* guy, Yourself.

**YOU MUST CHOOSE!**

Are you...

a **Mac** or **PC**?

a **Dog** or **Cat**?

**Salt** or **Pepper**?

**Abbott** or **Costello**?

**Sugar** or **Spice**?

**Day** or **Night**?

a **Beach** or **Mountain**?

**Doo-doo** or **Pee-pee**?

**YOU MUST CHOOSE!**

# If you were a **gem** or **precious stone**, what would you be?

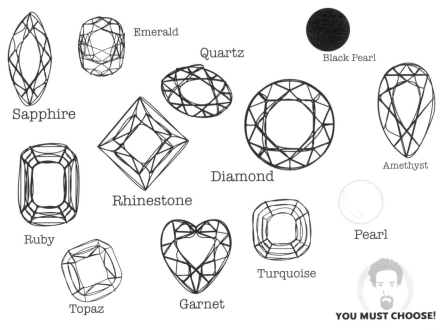

Emerald

Quartz

Black Pearl

Sapphire

Diamond

Amethyst

Rhinestone

Ruby

Pearl

Turquoise

Topaz

Garnet

**YOU MUST CHOOSE!**

9

# You Are What You Eat!

## If you were a **bar drink** or **cocktail**, what would you be?

Things to consider: Are you strong? Watered down? Fruity?

## If you were a **condiment**, what would you be?

## If you were a **dessert**, what would you be? What would the nutrition label say?

## If you were a **cereal**, which would you be? How about if you were a cereal mascot?

Things to consider: Why are all cereal mascots either addicts or pushers?

**YOU MUST CHOOSE!**

If you were a **cartoon character**, who would you be?

If you were a **deodorant scent**, what would you be?
Things to consider: alpine frost, cool breeze, clean blast, tundratastic, salmon

If you were an **exclamation** or **sound made during sex**, what would you be? (Say it like you mean it!)

If you were an **onomatopoeia** (a sound-word like SMACK, THUD, SPLAT, or SQUISH), what would you be?
Things to consider: We hope your answer to this question was not the same as the answer to the previous question.

**YOU MUST CHOOSE!**

Who is this actor?

If he were an **animal**, he'd be a fox.

If he were an **article of clothing**, he'd be a tailored suit.

If he were a **drink**, he'd be a martini.

If he were a **movie character**, he'd be James Bond.

Answer on page 164

**What Would You Be?**

If you were any **character from a movie** or **TV show**, who would you be?

If you were a **part of the body**, what would you be?

If you were a **shape**, what would you be? (Draw it.)

If you were any **famous John**, which John would you be?

Things to consider: Do you have a macho Western air about you? Does sunshine on your shoulders make you happy? Do you have large genitals? Do you have mutilated genitals?

If you were a **famous Jen** or **Jennifer**, who would you be?

**YOU MUST CHOOSE!**

13

If you were a **speed limit**, what would you be?

If you were a **type of terrain** (mountains, desert, foothills, etc.), what would you be?

If you were a **piece of furniture**, what would you be?

Things to consider: Are you leather? Worn down? Modern? Classic?

If you were a **candy bar**, what would you be?

Did you know?

*The Charleston Chew was invented by the Nazis as a battle snack.**

*Not true.

**YOU MUST CHOOSE!**

If you were a **musical instrument**, what would you be?

If you were a **musical note** or **chord**, what would you sound like? (Hum the note or play it if an instrument is near.)

Express who you are in a **drum solo**.

Express who you are by 20 seconds of **air guitar**.

**YOU MUST CHOOSE!**

If you were a **zoo animal**, what would you be?

If you were a **circus act**, what would you be?

If you were **something in Australia**, what would you be?

If you were a **Greek god**, who would you be?

*Question of character:*

What would you want to be **God of** if you could be God of something? Fashion? Flatulence? Bad Hair Days? First Dates? Ennui?

**YOU MUST CHOOSE!**

# Gone Hollywood

If you were a **movie**, what movie would you be?
Some ideas: *When Harry Met Sally, Friday the 13th, Rocky,
Pulp Fiction, Big Breast Bangers 8, Big Breast Bangers 9*.

If you were an **actor/actress**, who would you be?

If you were a **Hollywood super couple**, who would you be?

Things to consider: TomKat, Brangelina, Bennifer, Fabioprah.

*Question of character:*

If your life were to get an **Oscar nomination**, what would it
be for? Best actor? Best supporting actor?
Best writing? Best score? Special effects?

**YOU MUST CHOOSE!**

If you were a **hairstyle**, what would you be?

Some (but not all) to choose from:

### Crew cut
Says: All business.

### Spiked Mohawk
Says: "F off."

### Mullet
Says: Business in the front. Party in the back.

### The Visor
Says: Party in the front. Business in the back.

### The Afro
Says: Party everywhere.

18

**Pony tail.** Says: (for women) – **I'm playful and energetic.** (for men) – **I'm sensitive and trying to get laid.**

**The Anchorman** Says: **That shouldn't be a problem.**

**Middle part** Says: **Precision, symmetry. 1983.**

**Jheri Curls** Says: **It all.**

**YOU MUST CHOOSE!**

If you were a **month**, what would you be?

If you were a **playing card**, what would you be?

If you were a **country**, what would you be?

If you were a **sound**, what would you be?
Things to consider: a foghorn, a last gasp, glass breaking, wind chimes, gong

**YOU MUST CHOOSE!**

20

# Origa-ME

Tear this page out and make an **origami** (folded paper sculpture) that represents you.

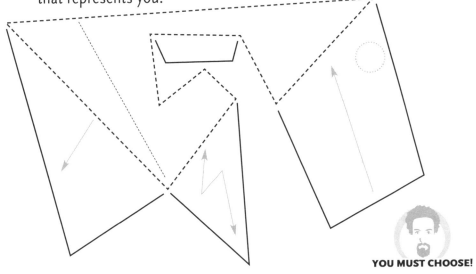

**YOU MUST CHOOSE!**

# Animal Instincts

If you were a **creature of the sea**, what would you be?

If you were a **mammal**, what would you be?

If you were an **insect**, what would you be?

If you were a **bird**, what would you be?

If you could create an **animal** that was you, what would it be?
Head of a _____? Body of a _____? Hands/claws of a
_____? Mind of a _____? Courage of a _____?

**YOU MUST CHOOSE!**

Are you...

a **fork**, **knife**, or **spoon**?

**rock**, **paper**, or **scissors**?

a **red**, **yellow**, or **green light**?

a **yes**, **no**, or **maybe**?

**Larry**, **Curly**, or **Moe**?

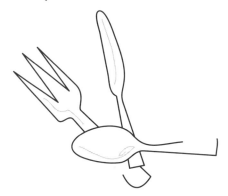

**YOU MUST CHOOSE!**

**If you were a song**, what song would you be? Which rendition? (Sing it.)

**If you were a spice**, what would you be?

**If you were a Spice Girl**, which would you be?

**If you were a famous historical figure**, who would you be?

Did you know?

*Confederacy President Jefferson Davis invented the high five.\**

\*Not true.

**YOU MUST CHOOSE!**

If you were a **hand tool**, what would you be?

If you were a **flower** or **plant**, what would you be?

If you were a **character in the Bible**, which would you be?

If you were a **video game character**, what character would you be?

*Question of character:*

What if you were a **character in a video game based on the Bible**? How would the game go? You get points for all the lepers you heal? All the suffering you can bear? All the outdated passages you interpret literally?

**YOU MUST CHOOSE!**

25

# You Are What You Write

If you were **handwriting**, what would you be?  Write a sentence in the handwriting that captures your essence.

If you were a **work of abstract art**, what would you be? (Draw it.)

If you were an **Instant Message acronym** (LOL, BRB, TTYL, etc.), what would you be?

*IM acronyms for super villains:  MLOL (Maniacal laugh out loud);* IWDY (I will destroy you); (BRBBYW) (Be right back, but you won't); ISSATEIAFIRFIWAANWIMOIE (I shall sweep away the Earth in a fiery inferno, recreating from its windblown ashes a new world in my own image everlasting)

**YOU MUST CHOOSE!**

### If you were a **planet**, which one would you be?

Things to consider: the beauty and mystique of Saturn, Jupiter the gas giant, the tempestuous and hot Venus, Uranus.

### If you were a **metal**, what would you be?

Things to consider: Are you strong? Lustrous? Precious?

### If you were a **curse word**, what would you be? How would you be said? (Demonstrate.)

### If you were a **monster**, what would you be?

Things to consider: vampire, zombie, yeti, black pudding, pubic elves, (See "About the Author" for the monster called Gomberg).

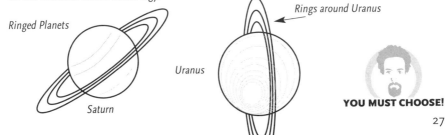

*Ringed Planets*

*Rings around Uranus*

*Uranus*

*Saturn*

**YOU MUST CHOOSE!**

## Who is this celebrity?

If he were a **food**, he'd be cheese.

If he were a **color**, he'd be gold.

If he were a **playing card**, he'd be the Ace of Spades.

If he were a **character from a movie**, he'd be Gordon Gekko.

Answer on page 164

If you were a **Smurf**, who would you be?

If you were **one of the seven dwarves**, which would you be?

If you were **one of the symptoms** Nyquil is meant to help with, which would you be?

If you were a **kickball pitch** ("slow and smooth", "fast and bouncy", etc.), what would you be?

*Ambivalent Smurf*

**YOU MUST CHOOSE!**

If you were a **time of the day**, what would you be?

If you were any **character from a book**, who would you be?

Things to consider: Holden Caulfield, Frodo Baggins, Scout, Encyclopedia Brown, Hamlet, Flat Stanley

If you were a **type of building** (hut, skyscraper, wigwam, office park), what would you be?

If you were a **comic strip character**, who would you be?

Things to consider: Dilbert, Garfield, Prince Valiant, Calvin, a *Far Side* cow, the *Would You Rather...?* guy (see the book *Would You Rather...? Illustrated* at wouldyourather.com).

**YOU MUST CHOOSE!**

If you were a **part of a Swiss Army knife**,
what would you be?

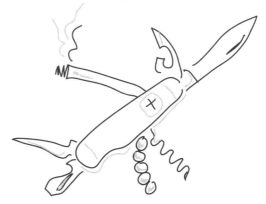

*Question of character:*

If you could design your own **personal Swiss army
knife**, what would you have on it? Some ideas:
an inhaler, breath spray, floss, a mirror, anal beads,
a cigarette, etc.

**YOU MUST CHOOSE!**

## If you were an **element of the periodic table**,
what would you be?

Things to consider: Are you stable? Volatile? Are you precious? Inert? Nerdy enough to like this question?

## If you were a **snack food**, what would you be?

## If you were a **texture**, what would you be?

*Question of character:*

If you had a **vanity plate** on your car, what would you have?
(Examples: IMCOOL, WADEVA, 2MUCH, ILUVSOD, etc.)

**YOU MUST CHOOSE!**

## Which one of you...

Which one of you or your friends is **Q-bert**?

Which one of you or your friends is a **desert**?

Which one of you or your friends is a **ruby**?

Which one of you or your friends is **The Fonz**?

Which one of you or your friends is **Swing dance**?

If you were a **book genre** what would you be?

If you were a **morning beverage**, what would you be?

### If you were **one of the founding fathers**,
who would you be?

Things to consider: the quiet but brilliant James Madison; the inflexible but eloquent Jefferson, the bold and commanding Washington, the bloated and problem-flatulent Templeton.

Did you know?

*The reason John Hancock signed his name larger than normal on the Declaration of Independence is because he had hands twice the size of a normal human being.\**

\*Not true. The real reason he signed so big was because he was an asshole.

**YOU MUST CHOOSE!**

# Life's a Gamble

If you were a **casino game**, what would you be?

How about if you were a **blackjack hand**?

## A poker hand?

## A roll of the dice in Craps?

And finally, finish this **slot machine spin**:
Cherry... Cherry... and...

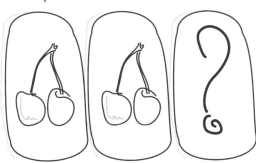

**YOU MUST CHOOSE!**

*Question of character:*

## What's in a Name?

Choose a **name** that best expresses your essence:

If you had a **rapper name**, what would it be?

If you had a **porn star name**, what would it be?

If you had a **pirate name**, what would it be?

If you had a ***Dungeons & Dragons* name**, what would it be?

If you had a **Mafia name**, what would it be?

**YOU MUST CHOOSE!**

If you were a **type of vehicle**, what would you be?

If you were a **street in New York City**, what would you be? Describe it in detail.

Things to consider: Wall Street, Park Avenue, a street in the West Village, a Harlem alley.

If you were a **famous landmark**, what would you be?

If you were a **smell**, what would you be?

Things to consider: roses, suntan oil, mulch, tar, new sheets, ass, BBQ, all of the above.

**YOU MUST CHOOSE!**

If you were a **three course meal**, what would you be? Describe each dish in detail as if on a menu.

**Appetizer?**

**First Course?**

**Main Course?**

**Side Dishes?**

**Dessert?**

If you were a *Star Wars* **character**, which one would you be?

If you were a **sandwich**, what would you be? (steak and cheese, club, sloppy joe, BLT, etc.)

If you were a **high school class**, what would you be?

If you were a **heart beat**, how would you beat?

## Mini-**Quiz**

*Star Wars* character **or** Extreme Sports Term?
   a. Jibber   b. Endo   c. Oola   d. Zyoh   e. Amaiza

Answers: a. slang for snowboarder; b. slang for being forcibly ejected from a bike over your handlebars; c. *Star Wars*, green-skinned slave of Jabba the Hutt; d. slang for "risk-taker"; e. *Star Wars*, former den-mother of the Black Hole Gang

**YOU MUST CHOOSE!**

# America's Game

**If you were a baseball position**, which would you be?

**If your life were a baseball at-bat** (home run, single, strike out, walk, reached base on error, bunt, foul, ground-rule double, etc.), what would you be?

**If you were a baseball pitch**, which would you be? (a fastball high and inside, knuckleball, etc.)

**If you were a baseball team**, which would you be?

**YOU MUST CHOOSE!**

If you were a **drug**, what would you be?

If you were a **national park**, what would you be?

If you were any **person who has been a reality show contestant**, who would you be?

If you were an **army man**, what would you be?

Things to consider: Bazooka guy, walkie-talkie guy, medic, bayonetter, etc.

**YOU MUST CHOOSE!**

*Question of character:*

## Super Being

**If you were turned into a superhero** (an original one), who would you be?

**What would your superpowers** be? For example, a lazy person you know might have the powers of sleeping through anything, deafening snore, and have projectile acidic drool.

**Who would your arch-enemy** be?

**What would your secret vulnerability** be?

**YOU MUST CHOOSE!**

If you were a **romantic act**, what would you be?
Examples: a soft kiss, a firm butt squeeze, an "accidental" brush and grope on the subway

If you were a **section of the newspaper**, what would you be?

If you were a **bodily function**, what would you be?

If you were a **poem**, what kind of poem you be? Would you rhyme? Any specific poem? Do you even know any specific poems? You disgust me.

**YOU MUST CHOOSE!**

If you were a **wedding ring**, what would you be?

If you were an **amateur sport** (field hockey, ping pong, Greco-Roman wrestling, etc.), what would you be?

If you were a **sky** (cloudy, clear blue, dusk, etc.), what would you be?

If you were a **vegetable**, what would you be?

**YOU MUST CHOOSE!**

If you were a **company**, what would you be?

If you were **something that goes in the mouth**, what would you be?

If you were a **cooking technique** (grilling, broiling, slow-cook, etc.), what would you be?

If you were any **palindrome** (race car, mom, dad, etc.), what would you be?

**YOU MUST CHOOSE!**

# Your True Character

If you were a **character from *Harry Potter***, who would you be?

If you were a **character from *Lost***, who would you be?

If you were a **character from *Heroes***, who would you be?

If you were a **character from *Sex and the City***, who would you be?

If you were a **character from *Grey's Anatomy***, who would you be?

**YOU MUST CHOOSE!**

### If you were a **Starbucks order**, what would you be?
(Give a detailed order.)

Things to consider: Are you decaf? Skim? Size? Iced? Latte?

### If you were a **jungle animal**, what would you be?

### If you were a **kind of massage**, what would you be?
(Demonstrate if needed.)

Things to consider: Would you be forceful? Gentle? An erotic massage? A neurotic massage?

*Question of character:*

**Would you ever give or receive a "Happy Ending" massage?** A Happy Beginning? A Melancholy Middle?

**YOU MUST CHOOSE!**

**What Would You Be?**

If you were a **tree**, what would you be?

If you were a **coin**, which coin would you be?

If you were a **piece of gardening equipment**, what would you be?

If you were any **alien as depicted in science fiction**, what would you be?

Things to consider: The ferocious creature in *Alien*, the seemingly benign but ultimately evil reptiles from *V*, Jawas, the ultralogical *Star Trek* super race susceptible to being defeated by paradox.

**YOU MUST CHOOSE!**

## Setting the Bar

If you were a **type of bar**, what would you be?
Describe your:

## **Décor and lighting**?

**Clientele**? What sort of conversations do they have?
Are there fights?

What do you serve? **What sort of neighborhood** are you located in?

What **music** is playing? Any other details?

What are you **named**?

**YOU MUST CHOOSE!**

### If you were a **character from *Peanuts***, who would you be?

Things to consider: Are you balding? Do you neglect your personal hygiene to the point of being a health hazard? Do you need a security blanket? Are you a Butch lesbian? Do you hold things out for people and suddenly take them away?

### If you were a **foreign language**, what would you be?

### If you were an **obscene gesture**, what would you be? (Demonstration optional.)

### If you were a **period in history**, which period would you be?

**YOU MUST CHOOSE!**

# Quiz 3

## Who is this famous person?

If he were an **animal**, he might be a hyena. Though a few would claim he is a lion.

If he were a **weapon**, he'd be a whip or maybe a Colt 45.

If he were a **tool**, he'd be a hammer.

If he were a **key on the keyboard**, detractors would say he'd be the Delete key. Supporters would say he's the Enter key.

If he were a **punctuation mark**, he'd be an exclamation mark.

Answer on page 164

What Would You Be?

# If you were a **road sign**, what would you be?

**YOU MUST CHOOSE!**

If you were a **reptile** or **amphibian**, what would you be?

If you were a **commercial slogan** ("Just Do It", "Sometimes you feel like a nut...", "I'm not gonna pay a lot for this muffler...", "Keeps on going and going and going...", etc.), what would you be?

If you were a **character from *Friends***, which would you be?

If you were an **over-the-counter medication**, what would you be?

Did you know?

*Matt LeBlanc has two club feet.** *

*Not true.

**YOU MUST CHOOSE!**

# Web You.0

If you were a **website**, what would you be?

If you were a **download speed**, what would you be? Does your connection go out a lot?

If you were a **spider web**, what would you look like? Draw it. What if Charlotte from *Charlotte's Web* made a web to represent you?

*Question of character:*

If you started typing "po..." in a web browser, what is most likely to pop up from frequent use: popsugar.com, pornocentral.com, or polygonsrcool.net? Check your browser and see.

**YOU MUST CHOOSE!**

If you were a **Monopoly property** (Boardwalk, Baltic Avenue, etc.), what would you be?

If you were an **extinct animal**, what would you be?

If you were a **number between one and ten**, what number would you be?

Things to consider: What number gets laid the most? What number is the biggest asshole? What is the most beautiful number? The most mysterious? The most pelborp?

If you were an **item in the supermarket**, what would you be?

*Question of character:*

What are the first five items on your shopping list?
What would never be on it?

**YOU MUST CHOOSE!**

55

Are you...

**Paula**, **Randy**, or **Simon**?

**87**, **89**, or **93 gasoline**?

**Boxers**, **briefs**, or **nothing**?

**Firemen**, **police**, or **paramedics**?

a **shot**, **assist**, or **rebound**?

**YOU MUST CHOOSE!**

If you were **something in a yard**, what would you be?

If you were **something in a mall**, what would you be?

If you were **something in Washington, D.C.**, what would you be?

If you were **something in the closet**, what would you be?

**YOU MUST CHOOSE!**

**What Would You Be?**

If your boss were a **movie villain**, which one would he/she be?

If your boss were an **amusement park ride**, which one would he/she be?

If your boss were a **piece of e-mail spam**, what would the subject line say?

If your boss were a **tourist attraction**, which would he/she be?

Are you ...

a **consonant** or a **vowel**?

a **thrust** or a **parry**?

**Bert** or **Ernie**?

**Dr. Jekyll** or **Mr. Hyde**?

a **whisper** or a **shout**?

**YOU MUST CHOOSE!**

# Fantasy Football

If you were a **position in football**, what would you be?

If your life were a **football play** (sack, touchdown, reverse, blocked punt, Hail Mary, etc.), which would you be? Bonus: Do the commentary of four downs that embody your life.

If you were an **NFL team**, what team would you be and why? Examples: A Bengal: good-looking uniform (body), ugly helmet (face.)

If you were a **football penalty**, what would you be?

*Question of character:*

If you had to do a **post-touchdown celebration** that personifies you, what would you do? (Demonstrate it.)

**YOU MUST CHOOSE!**

If you were a **song from the early eighties**, what song would you be?

If you were a **cut of steak**, what cut would you be? How would you be cooked? Seasoned?

If you were a **sitcom character**, who would you be?

*Question of character:*

If you had an **original sitcom catchphrase**, what would it be? Some ideas: ... "Uh, NO THANK YOU!"; "That's a little more info than I need to knooooowwwwwwwww!"; "Guess you had to be there"; "Indeeditron 2000!"; and "Sheeeeeyit!"

**YOU MUST CHOOSE!**

# Sumpin' Sumpin'

If you were **something with wheels**, what would you be?

If you were **something with wings**, what would you be?

If you were **something on a farm**, what would you be?

If you were **something in the kitchen**, what would you be?

Things to consider: Can you think of an object that satisfies all of the above? If so, email the answer to **info@wouldyourather.com**, subject heading: "Too much time on my balls." So far, the best we have is a partially formed chicken in an egg (but no wheels).

**YOU MUST CHOOSE!**

If you were a **Disney character**, what would you be?

If you were a **gun**, what would you be?

If you were a **mythical creature**, what would you be?

If you were an **architectural style**, what would you be?

*Question of character:*

If *Disney on Ice* put on an ice show of your life, how would that go?

**YOU MUST CHOOSE!**

### If you were a **mode of transportation**, what would you be?

### If you were an **email command**, what would you be?

Things to consider: reply, forward, delete, archive, send, keep as new

### If you were a **store**, what would you be?

### If you were a **magic spell**, what would you be?

Things to consider; invisibility, forcefield, fireball, freeze, levitate, turn to stone, poison, prismatic lights, cure wounds.

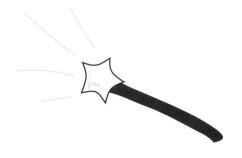

**YOU MUST CHOOSE!**

If you were a **disease**, what would you be?

If you were a **culture from history** (Aztec, Vikings, Cherokee, etc.), what would you be?

If you were a **bumper sticker**, what would you be?

If you were a **button on your TV remote**, what would you be?

**YOU MUST CHOOSE!**

## 20 Stupid Questions

Take a break from *WWYB* to play this game. If in a public place, pick someone you don't know, but that each of you can see. If not in a public place, think of a well-known celebrity or historical figure. Then play 20 questions, but use only these questions of conjecture. One player pick the person, the other ask. After asking/answering these questions, guess who the person is. Indeeditron 2000.

- Could you see this person secretly liking to be tied up and dominated?

- Does this person misspell "maintenance"?

- If this person was in a fight with John Larroquette, would they win?

- Is this person a farter?

- Does this person sing in the shower? On the toilet?

- Does he/she have a good voice?

- Does this person like penguins?

- Do these pants make my butt look big?

**YOU MUST CHOOSE!**

If you were a **donut**, what would you be? What if you were a **doughnut**?

If you were a **president**, who would you be?

If you were a **decade**, which decade would you be?

If you were a **TV channel**, what would you be?

Did you know?

*John Quincy Adams was the world's first bisexual.\**

*Not true

**YOU MUST CHOOSE!**

If you were a **kiss**, what would you be?
(Demonstrate on your hand.)

If you were **foreplay**, what would you be?
(Demonstrate on your forearm.)

If you were a **form of sexual intercourse**, what would you be? (Demonstrate on the throw pillow or couch corner.)

*Question of character:*

What is the **weirdest sexual dream** you've ever had?

**YOU MUST CHOOSE!**

# Getting Specific

## Fill the crap out of these blanks!

I am a _____ that is being _____ _____
       (insert sporting equipment)            (insert sports action)   (adverb)

by _____ .
     (insert plural noun)

Sample answer: I am a ping-pong ball that is being paddled madly by relatives.

I am a/an _____ in a pile of _____ that is about to be
      (insert noun)           (insert noun)

_____ by a/an _____ _____ .
 (insert verb)             (insert adjective)     (insert noun)

Sample answer: I am a crouton in a pile of lettuce that is about to be eaten by an angry vegetarian.

**YOU MUST CHOOSE!**

69

If you were a **beer**, what would you be?

If you were an **occupation**, what would you be?

If you were a **height**, which one would you be?

If you were a **drunken antic**, what would you be? Act it out.

Things to consider: being over-friendly, getting into a fight, dropping pants, talking too much like Loose Lips Schirtz.

**YOU MUST CHOOSE!**

If you were a **basketball shot**, what would you be (Examples: Short-range jump hook, Two-handed tomahawk dunk, Fade-away 3-pointer)? Does your shot go in?

If you were a **famous singer**, who would you be?

If you were a **school supply**, what would you be?

If you were a **dance style**, what would you be (tap, break-dancing, ballet, square-dancing, etc.)?

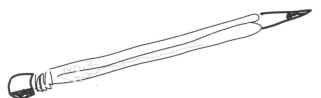

**YOU MUST CHOOSE!**

# Acting Out

If you were a **talent show act**, what would it be?
(Demonstrate it.)

If you were a **70's song**, which would it be? (Sing it.)

If you were a **quote from a movie**, what would it be? (Say it.)

If you were a **scene from a movie**, which would it be?
(Mime it.)

**YOU MUST CHOOSE!**

**If you were a street, what would you be?**

**If you were a fashion accessory, what would you be?**

**If you were a soda, what would you be?**

### If you were a classic arcade game character, what would you be?

Things to consider: Are you a glutton that loves the thrill of the chase? Do you have a hero streak and a propensity to dodge barrels either literally or metaphorically? Are you prone to diagonal hopping and unidentifiably punctuated profanity?

**YOU MUST CHOOSE!**

If you were a **fashion label**, which one would you be?

If you were a **restaurant chain**, which would you be?

If you were a **part of speech**, which would you be?

If you were a **spread that you put on bread** (mayonnaise, margarine, peanut butter, Vegemite, marshmallow fluff, etc.), what would you be?

**YOU MUST CHOOSE!**

# Graph your life.

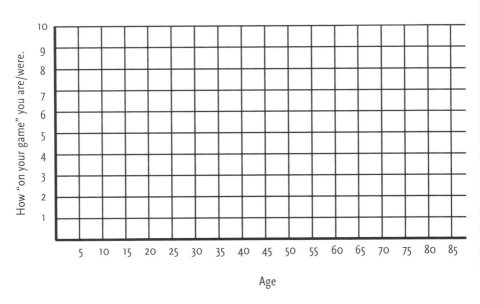

How "on your game" you are/were.

Age

If you were a **fish**, what would you be?

If you were a **dance move**, what would you be?
(Demonstrate it.)

If you were any **liquid**, what would you be?

If you were a **form of communication** (mime, speech, sign language, email, etc.) what would you be?

Did you know?

*There is a tribe in the Amazon that communicates solely in taint-scratching?**

*This is true.

**YOU MUST CHOOSE!**

*Make Your Own Movie*

Combine the elements to create a movie that best represents you:

**Genre**?

**Setting**?

**Leading Actor**?

**Leading Actress**?

**Soundtrack**?

If you were a **character on the following TV shows**, who would you be?

*The Office?*

*Beverly Hills 90210?*

*Happy Days?*

*Gilligan's Island?*

*The Facts of Life?*

**YOU MUST CHOOSE!**

If you were an **internal organ**, what would you be?

If you were **something in space**, what would you be?

If you were a **"diet"** (Atkins, Zone, South Beach, Fudge only, etc.), what would you be?

---

**New diet idea:** *The Progressively Difficult Utensil Diet®*
You can eat as much as you want, but you have to use the utensil specified. Chopsticks for breakfast with cereal, ladles for lunch with a roast beef sandwich. A round rubber ball for a turkey and mashed potato dinner. It is so hard to eat in any big quantity, you'll lose weight.

**YOU MUST CHOOSE!**

# What are you made of?

Fill the bejesus out of these blanks to make the recipe of **You**.

**You**:

Two tablespoons of _____.

A liter of _____.

Action (stir, shake, blend, etc.) _____.

Add a dash of_____.

Garnish with _____.

**YOU MUST CHOOSE!**

If you were a **Dr. Seuss character**, what would you be?

If you were a **Microsoft Word feature**, what would you be?

If you were a **hotel**, which hotel would you be?

Things to consider: The Four Seasons, Holiday Inn, Merle's Inn by the Hour, etc.

If you were a **method of execution**, what would you be?

"Seuss in a Noose"

**YOU MUST CHOOSE!**

If you were a **high school clique**, what would you be?

If you were a **magazine**, what would you be?

If you were a **city in California**, what would you be?

If you were a **piece of jewelry**, what would you be?
Some to choose from: diamond earrings, Indian charm necklace, pearl necklace.

Some more to choose from: helium balloon earrings, fish weight and bobber scrotal piercing, rapper-style grill.

**YOU MUST CHOOSE!**

**If you were a restaurant**, what would you be?

**If you were a pasta**, what would you be?

**If you were a children's book**, what would you be?

**If you were a nonsense word**, what would you be?
Some ideas: Barg! Flimp! Prazeo. Queese. Ronk! Siff.

Open all night

Siff's Pizza

Parking in rear

**YOU MUST CHOOSE!**

# Golf Lundgren*

What **golf club** are you?

Are you a **par 3**, **4**, or **5**?

A **birdie**, **bogey**, or **par**?

If you were **part of a golf course**, what would you be?

Things to consider: the rough, fairway, putting green, sandtrap, fringe.

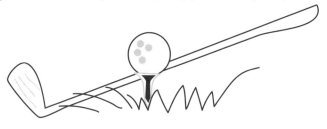

*(Voted Worst Pun, 2007, National Association of Punsters)

**YOU MUST CHOOSE!**

# If you were a **hat** or **piece of headwear**, what would you be?

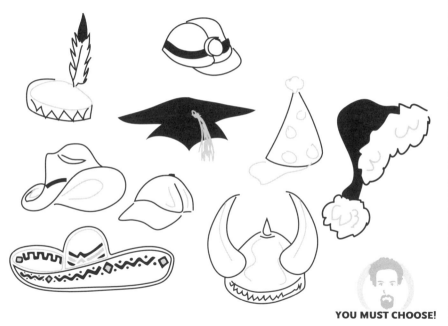

**YOU MUST CHOOSE!**

If you were a **farm animal**, what would you be?

If you were a **music album**, past or present, what would you be?

If you were a **famous building**, what would you be?

If you were a **romantic gesture**, what would you be?
How would you be executed?

**YOU MUST CHOOSE!**

Combine the elements to create a **sundae** that represents you...

**Ice cream flavor**?

**Hot Fudge**, **Caramel**, or **Strawberry**?

Additional **toppings**?

**Cherry** on top?  Or something else?

Give the **traffic report** that represents you. (Recite the report as if on the radio: "Gridlock, backed up for miles, possibly an accident, delays expected.")

If you were a type of **bag**, what would you be?

If you were a type of **deli meat**, what would you be?

If you were a piece of **playground equipment**, what would you be?

**YOU MUST CHOOSE!**

## Which one of you...

Which of you or your friends would be **Christmas**?

Which of you or your friends would be **denim**?

Which of you or your friends would be **milk and cookies**?

Which of you or your friends would be a **full moon**?

Which of you or your friends would be an **overhead smash**?

**If you were an emoticon**, which would you be?

0=)    </3    0-\-<]:

:-E

:_(    :(

(:|    ;-)

:*)    :->

*_*    :0)

**YOU MUST CHOOSE!**

If you were a **room** (study, office, bedroom, etc.), what would you be?

If you were a **laugh**, what would you be? (Laugh it.)

If you were a *Saved by the Bell* **character**, who would you be?

If you were a **Monopoly token**, what would you be?

**YOU MUST CHOOSE!**

If you were a **Village Person**, what would you be?

If you were a **type of pie**, what would you be?

If you were a **wine**, what would you be?

If you were a **driving violation** (speeding, parking by a hydrant, DWI, broken tail light, etc.), what would you be?

**YOU MUST CHOOSE!**

# Game On

**If you were a board game**, what would you be?
Some ideas: Twister, Yahtzee, Trivial Pursuit, Scrabble, etc.

**If you were a character in Clue**, who would you be?
Things to consider: Colonel Mustard, Professor Plum, Miss Scarlet, Miss Peacock

**If you were a piece in Stratego**, what would you be? If you don't know Stratego, which chess piece would you be?

**If you were a game show**, what would you be?

**YOU MUST CHOOSE!**

If you were a **genre of music**, what would you be?

If you were a **pattern** (stripe, polka dots, paisley, etc.), what would you be?

If you were a **fabric**, what would you be?

If you were a **martial art/style of fighting**, what would you be?

*Question of character:*

Describe a **kung fu movie** based on your life. What is the title? What is the plot? How and where do the fight scenes break out?

**YOU MUST CHOOSE!**

If you were a **Muppet**, who would you be?

If you were a **tie** (pattern, style, color, etc.), what would you be?

If you were a **type of cake**, what would you be?

If you were a ***Rocky* movie** (*1,2,3,4,5,* or *Rocky Balboa*), which would you be?

YOU MUST CHOOSE!

If your mom were a **natural disaster** (hurricane, tidal wave, etc.), what would she be?

If your mom were an **animal**, what would she be?

If your mom were a **fantasy race** (orc, troll, hobbit, elf, etc.) what would she be?

If your mom were a **movie character**, who would she be?

# Getting Juvenile

If you were a **fart**, what would you be? (Make the sound—unless you're the silent but deadly variety.)

If you were a **belch**, what would you be? (Make it count.)

If you were an **accent**, what would you be? (Try to read the next question in that accent.)

If you were a **sneeze**, what would you be? (Imitate it.)

*Question of character:*

Do you say "Bless you" to people? Do you like it?
Social experiment: Try saying "I will destroy you"
instead of "Bless you" when people sneeze and
see what happens.

**YOU MUST CHOOSE!**

If you were a **famous speech** (Gettysburg Address, I Have a Dream, Bill Murray riff in *Caddyshack*, Sermon on the Mount, *Hamlet* soliloquy, etc.), what would you be?

If you were a **type of alcohol**, what would you be?

If you were a **punch** (place, power, and style), what would you be? (Demonstrate it.)

If you were a **gymnastic maneuver or floor exercise**, what would you be? (Demonstration optional, not responsible for bodily injury.)

**YOU MUST CHOOSE!**

If you were an **outside temperature to the nearest degree**, what would you be?

If you were a **paper money denomination**, what would you be?

If you were a **New York neighborhood**, what would you be?

If you were a **neighborhood in your city or county**, what would you be?

YOU MUST CHOOSE!

If you were a **college**, what would you be?

If you were a **type of ethnic cuisine** (Italian, Mexican, etc.), what would you be?

If you were a **carnival ride**, what would you be?

If you were a **way of serving eggs**, what would you be?

Things to consider: scrambled, sunny side-up, raw, poached, with Tabasco, eggs Benedict, eggs Florentine, eggs Unseld

**YOU MUST CHOOSE!**

# If you were a **facial hair style**, what would you be?

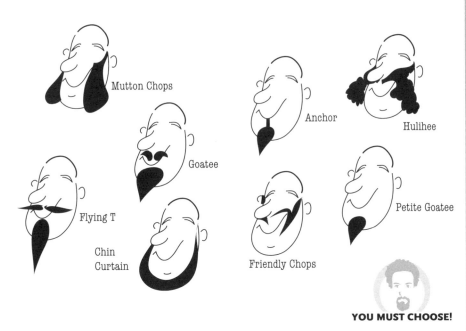

Mutton Chops

Anchor

Hulihee

Goatee

Flying T

Chin Curtain

Friendly Chops

Petite Goatee

**YOU MUST CHOOSE!**

101

If you were a **sea craft**, what would you be?

If you were a **material**, what would you be?

If you were a **sauce**, what would you be?

If you were a **weather phenomenon**, what would you be?

Did you know?

*Grey Poupon is lethal in large doses.*\*

\*Not true.

**YOU MUST CHOOSE!**

**If you were a week in a menstrual cycle,** what would you be?

**If you were a museum,** what would you be?

**If you were a sport,** what would you be?

**If you were a *Sesame Street* character,** who would you be?

Things to consider: Are you an addict and glutton? Are you obsessive-compulsive? Do you suffer from depression?

YOU MUST CHOOSE!

Are you...

**economy class, business class**, or **first class?**

**Doric, Ionic** or **Corinthian?**

**beef, fish**, or **chicken?**

**Yahoo, Google**, or **AOL?**

**Heaven, Hell**, or **Purgatory?**

**YOU MUST CHOOSE!**

**If you were a type of makeup** (i.e. black mascara, candy red lipstick, nail polish), what would you be?

**If you were an undergarment**, what would you be?
Describe in detail. Yes, describe in detail (heavy breathing.)

Things to consider: Lace bra, granny panties, chastity belt, crotchless panties.

**If you were a piece of gym equipment**, what would you be?

**If you were a fairy tale character**, who would you be?

**YOU MUST CHOOSE!**

If you were a **season**, which would you be?

If you were a **beverage**, what would you be?

If you were a **cough**, what would you be? (Cough it.)

If you were an **Olympic event**, what would you be?

Did you know?

*The Chinese government removes organs from their Olympic gymnasts and wrestlers to make them lighter.**

*Not true.

**YOU MUST CHOOSE!**

# You Are What You Read

**If you were a children's book character**, what/who would you be?

Things to consider: Lemony Snicket, The Grinch, Rudolph, Charlotte, Flat Stanley, Bigballs Franklin

**If you were any novel**, what would you be?

**If you were the first sentence of a book** (real or imagined), what would you be?

---

*3 Awful First Sentences to a Novel:*

The sunset spread across the sky like Athlete's Foot.

The pudding seemed to breathe.

She was all ligaments.

**YOU MUST CHOOSE!**

# It's Your Life

If your childhood was a **weather forecast**, what would it be?

If your family was a **rock band**, who would they be?

If your adolescence was a **beach report** (waves, riptide, etc.), what would it be?

If your neighborhood were an **orchestra**, who would be what instrument?

**YOU MUST CHOOSE!**

If you were a **whistle**, what would you be?

If you were a **made-up language**, what would you be? (Speak it.)

If you were a **book**, which would you be?

*Schirtzenfreude:*
Someone's Life
Is Always Tougher

*Falls Media*

*Question of character:*

**Give five chapter titles** of your memoirs were they to be written some day.

**YOU MUST CHOOSE!**

## If you were a **piece of sports equipment**,

what would you be?

**YOU MUST CHOOSE!**

If you were a **member of the opposite sex**,
who would you be?

If you were a **member of your own sex**, other than yourself,
who would you be?

If you were a **sports team**, what team would you be?

If you were a **message on a candy heart**,
what would you be?

Please do me

**YOU MUST CHOOSE!**

# Graph your life.

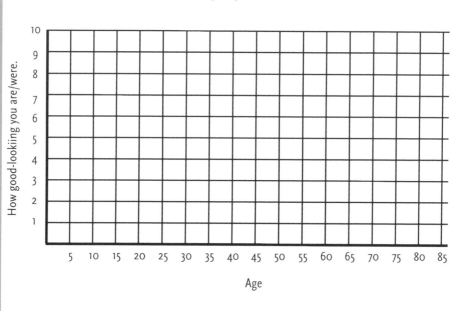

How good-looking you are/were.

Age

### If you were a **type of party** or **social gathering**, what would you be?

Things to consider: rave, cocktail party, Bar-mitzvah, orgy

### If you were a **Dungeons & Dragons class**, what would you be?

### If you were a **holiday**, what would you be?

### What about if you were a **holiday creature**?

Things to consider: Tooth Fairy, Easter Bunny, ground hog, Thanksgiving turkey, Santa Claus, Jesus, Lord of Brisket

**YOU MUST CHOOSE!**

## Who is this actress?

If she were a **weather forecast**, she'd be sunny and hot, with a chance of afternoon thunderstorms.

If she were a **flower**, she'd be a thorny, long-stemmed black rose.

If she were a **car**, she'd be a lipstick red Ferrari.

If she were a **Chinese food dish**, she'd be sweet and spicy stir fry.

Answer on page 164

**If you were a type of radio station**, what would you be? What would your call letters be?

**If you were part of a car**, what would you be?

**If you were a view from a window**, what would you be?

**If you were a house**, what would you be? What style? How many stories? Siding? Color? Do you have an open back door?

**YOU MUST CHOOSE!**

If you were a **fictional robot**, who would you be?

If you were an **extreme sport**, what would you be?

If you were a **criminal offense**, what would you be?

If you were **part of a boat**, what would you be?

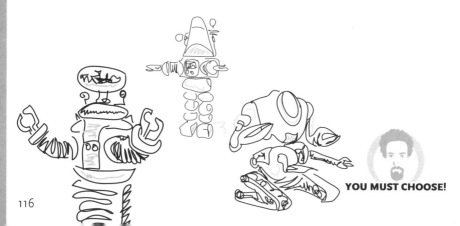

YOU MUST CHOOSE!

# Nerds Only

If you were a **linear equation**, what would you be?

If you were a **scientific compound**, what would you be?

If you were a **mathematical formula**, what would you be?

**Give your Dungeons & Dragons statistics** (strength, intelligence, wisdom, charisma, dexterity and constitution)? What is your alignment? Armor class? Psionic ability. I mean, what? I'm cool. Sports and girls, man.

$$\frac{-\pi \cdot x \angle bc + 24^{cx^{39}}}{(abcd)^{42}/3xy} \sqrt{\frac{gomberg}{heimberg}}$$

**YOU MUST CHOOSE!**

If you were a **tennis shot** (serve, smash, volley, backhand, forehand), what would you be? Are you in or out?

If you were a **shave** (smooth, lots of cuts, Miami Vice beard, razor burn, etc.), what would you be?

If you were a **type of mail delivery** (FedEx overnight, USPS First Class, bulk rate, etc.), what would you be?

If you were a **tech accessory**, what would you be?

**YOU MUST CHOOSE!**

# If you were a **type of footwear**, what would you be?

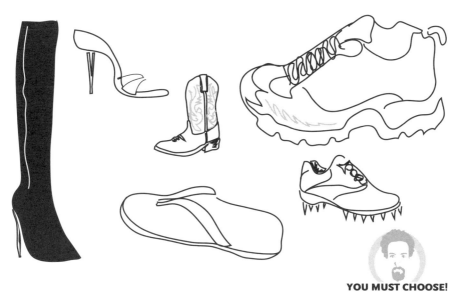

**YOU MUST CHOOSE!**

If you were a **band** or **musical act**, who would you be?

If you were a **common expression**, what would you be?

Things to consider: Hello, Goodbye, Thank you, You're welcome, Bless you, Where are my gold pants?

If you were a **famous historical criminal**, who would you be?

*Question of character:*

If you had a **band**, what would the **name** be? A few to consider: The Starch, Black Pancreas, Hobbit Pimp, Tubman. Look through this book to find a good band name (e.g. on the next page is the phrase "Seven Footer", a great name for a band. Same with "Razor Burn", a few pages earlier.)

**YOU MUST CHOOSE!**

## If you were a **comedian**, who would you be?

Things to consider: Dane Cook, Carrot Top, Dennis Miller, Chris Rock, David Spade, Adam Sandler, Seinfeld, Ellen, Poundstone (also a good band name), Jeff Foxworthy

## If you were a **type of computer**, what would you be?

## If you were a **former NBA seven footer**, who would you be?

## If you were a **constellation**, what would you be?

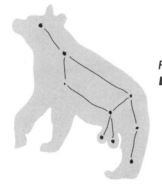

*Forgotten constellation:*
***Leonaris, the big-balled bear***

**YOU MUST CHOOSE!**

121

*"There are no time-outs in the world of professional wrestling"*

*— Winston Churchill*

If you were a **past** or **present professional wrestler**, who would you be?

If you were a **professional wrestling move** or **hold**, what would you be? Demonstrate it (carefully).

If your life were a **type of wrestling match**, what would it be (steel cage, street fight, tactical battle, lumberjack, tables, ladders and chairs, etc.)?

*Question of character:*

If you were a **made up professional wrestler**, who would you be (what name and gimmick)?

Things to consider: "The Barista", "The Existentialist", "The Sommelier"

**YOU MUST CHOOSE!**

If you were a **medical instrument**, what would you be?

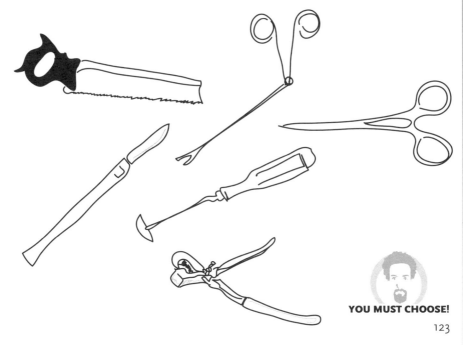

**YOU MUST CHOOSE!**

123

# Sibling Rivalry

If your brother/sister were a **type of joke** (riddle, pratfall, witty barb, a "not" joke, etc.), what would he/she be?

If your brother/sister were a ***Seinfeld* character**, which would he/she be?

If your brother/sister were a **cheerleader cheer**, what would he/she be?

If your brother/sister were a **Biblical quote**, **passage**, or **story**, what would he/she be?

**YOU MUST CHOOSE!**

**If you were a Dorito flavor**, what would you be?

Things to consider: Cool Ranch, Fiery Habanero, Reduced Fat, Smokin' Cheddar BBQ, Guacamole, Pizza Cravers

**If you were a letter**, which would you be? Are you capital or lower case?

**If you were a bra measurement**, what would you be?

**If you were a dress length**, what would you be?

Did you know?

*Doritos are shaped like triangles because of a powerful triangle lobby (Big Triangle).\**

\*Not true.

**YOU MUST CHOOSE!**

If you were a **basketball position**, what would you be?

If you were an **angle**, what would you be?

Things to consider: Are you acute? Obtuse? Right?

If you were a **chewing gum**, what would you be?

If you were a **bone**, what would you be?

**YOU MUST CHOOSE!**

**If you were potatoes** (fried, mashed, home fries, etc.), what would you be?

**If you were a type of literary device**, what would you be?

Things to consider: think back to 8th grade English: hyperbole, irony, metaphor, metonymy, alliteration, simple rhyming.

**Make a pizza** that represents you.

**Crust?**

**Cheese?**

**Toppings?**

**Size?**

**YOU MUST CHOOSE!**

# Fearsome Foursomes

Are you...

**bitter**, **salty**, **sour**, or **sweet**?

an "**if**", "**and**" "**or**" "**but**"?

**Groucho**, **Harpo**, **Chico**, or **Zeppo**?

**water**, **fire**, **earth**, or **air**?

**north**, **south**, **east**, or **west**?

**God**, **Jesus**, **The Holy Ghost**, or **Tom Kite**?

**YOU MUST CHOOSE!**

# Everyone was Feng Shui Lighting

Interior-decorate a room that represents you.

What is the **furniture**?

How is it **arranged**?

What is the **lighting**?

Describe the **walls**. **Ceiling**? **Floor**?

What is the **shape of the room**?

**YOU MUST CHOOSE!**

129

**If you were a religion**, what would you be?

**If you were a salad**, what would you be? Which type?
What ingredients? Dressing?

**If you were an omelet**, what would you be?

**If you were a good deed**, what would you be?

Did you know?

*The ultimate good deed doers, the Boy Scouts of
America, do not tolerate homosexuality despite
wearing ascots, pursuing craftwork, and
congregating in basements with groups
of boys and men.*

**YOU MUST CHOOSE!**

## Personal Transformation

**If you were a Transformer**, what would you transform into?

A few ideas: A Porsche, a jet, gun, a yarmulke, one of those foot-measuring devices, a George Foreman Grill, a whack-a-mole game

## Mini-**Quiz**

Muscle *or* Transformer?

a. Teres Major      b. Rodimus Prime

c. Omega Supreme      d. Lattissimus Dorsi

e. Supinator      f. Scorponok

Answers: Muscles: a, d, e.

**YOU MUST CHOOSE!**

131

**What Would You Be?**

If you were a **continent**, which would you be?

If you were an **'80s movie character**, who would you be?

If you were **sushi** or a **sushi roll**, what would you be?

If you were a **swim stroke**, what would you be?

Did you know?

*The water on the left side of the pool is always cooler than the water on the right side.**

*Come on. That doesn't even make sense.

**YOU MUST CHOOSE!**

**If you were a weapon**, what would you be?

**YOU MUST CHOOSE!**

133

If you were a **Broadway play**, what would you be?

If you were a **rainfall** (storm, gentle shower, etc.), what would you be?

If you were an **age**, what would you be?

If you were a **1960's cultural icon**, who would you be?

**YOU MUST CHOOSE!**

134

# Acting Out

Act out a **mime routine** (charades) of your life.

Act out an **interpretive dance** of your life.

Act out an **opera** of your life.

Act out a **porno** of your life.

Act out a **porno-opera** of your life.

**YOU MUST CHOOSE!**

# Your Better Half

If you're not married, read "spouse" as "boyfriend" or "girlfriend". If you don't have one of those, read it as "crush", and if you don't have one of those, read it as "I need to get out more."

If your spouse was a **body of water**, what would he/she be?

If your spouse was a **play-date between 3rd graders**, what would he/she be?

If your spouse was a **horned animal**, what would he/she be?

If your spouse was a **talent show act**, what would he/she be?

**YOU MUST CHOOSE!**

**Pretend to drive your personality.**

Or if in a car, actually drive your personality (without crashing).

**If you were a Justice League member**, who would you be?

**If you were a rodeo event**, what would you be?

**If you were a type of tea**, what would you be?

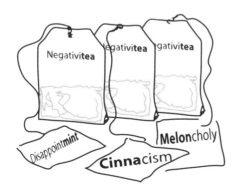

Negativitea

Negativitea

Negativitea

Disappointmint

Cinnacism

Meloncholy

**YOU MUST CHOOSE!**

137

If you were a **member of the Rat Pack**, who would you be?
(Sinatra, Sammy Davis, Jr., Dean Martin)

If you were a **member of the Brat Pack**, who would you be?
(Judd Nelson, Emilio Estevez, Andrew McCarthy, Molly Ringwald, Ally Sheedy, etc.)

If you were a **member of the Frat Pack**, who would you be?
(Will Ferrell, Wilson Brothers, Ben Stiller, Vince Vaughn, etc.)

If you were a **member of the Scat Pack**, who would you be?

**YOU MUST CHOOSE!**

# Toys

**If you were a kid's toy**, what would you be? (Slinky, jacks, Barbie, Vortex football, Silly Putty, Serious Putty, Putty Whose Level of Frivolity Varies from Day to Day)

**If you were an adult toy**, what would you be? (vibrator, lube, nipple clamp, triple ripple butt plug, whip, etc.)

**If you were a children's game**, what would you be?

**If you were a Rubik's cube**, how would you be arranged?

**YOU MUST CHOOSE!**

139

If you were a **track and field event**, what would you be?

If you were a **summer camp activity**, what would you be?

If you were a **pick-up line**, what would you be?

If you were an **Indian tribe**, what would you be? Or any tribe for that matter.

Things to consider: There are lots of summer camps with a Native American theme that Jewish families send their kids too. But what about the reverse? A camp with a Jewish theme that Native American families can send their kids to. Please send ideas for crafts and activities to info@wouldyourather.com.

**YOU MUST CHOOSE!**

# Character Counts

If you were a **character from *Lord of the Rings***, who would you be?

If you were a ***Scooby Doo* character**, who would you be?

If you were a ***Star Trek* character**, who/what would you be?

If you were a **soap opera character**, who would you be?

If you were an ***X-Men* member**, who would you be?

**YOU MUST CHOOSE!**

# If you were an **article of clothing**, what would you be?

**YOU MUST CHOOSE!**

If you were a **type of bagel**, what would you be?

If you were a **primate**, what would you be?

If you were an **office** or **office station at work**, what would you be? Describe it. Are you a cubicle with a poster of a kitty? A corner office with a mahogany desk?

If you were a **type of fetish porn**, what would you be?

*Can you combine all of the above into one image?*
*If so, draw and submit it to info@wouldyourather.com.*

**YOU MUST CHOOSE!**

If you were a **cat breed**, what would you be?

If you were a **Microsoft Word template**, what would you be?

Are you a **sunset** or a **sunrise**?

If you were a **type of shirt**, what would you be?
What's the style? Brand? Fit?

Did you know?

*Tommy Hilfiger's real name is Merle Klendledorf.**

*Totally false.

**YOU MUST CHOOSE!**

**Encapsulate yourself in one breath.**

**If you were a timepiece, what would you be?**
Things to consider: stopwatch, grandfather clock, hourglass, Rolex, etc.

**If you were a college class, what would you be?**

**If you were a Beatles song** (in terms of both words and melody), what would you be?

**YOU MUST CHOOSE!**

# Picking You Apart

If your voice was a **texture**, what would it be?

If your mind was a **landscape photograph**, what would it be?

If your heart and soul were a **color**, what would it be?

If your demeanor were a **plane flight**, what would it be?

If your nerves were a **substance**, what would they be?

**YOU MUST CHOOSE!**

*Question of character:*

## Make It Up

If your life were a **Dr. Seuss book**, what would it be called?

If your life were a **video game**, what would it be called?
Describe how it would be played. What would you score points for?

If your life were a **Jon Krakauer book**, what would it
be called?

If your life were a **Disney World ride**, what would it be
called? Describe how it would go. Would it make people sick?

**YOU MUST CHOOSE!**

If you were a **vacation**, what would you be?

If you were a **touch to the face** (caress, slap, "got your nose", cheek pinch, etc.), what would you be? (Demonstrate on someone.)

If you were a **TV host** or **anchorperson**, who would you be?

If you were a **poster**, what would you be?

*Question of character:*

What did you have on your walls growing up? In college? What's the dumbest or most embarrassing thing you had?

**YOU MUST CHOOSE!**

# Time Goes By

If you were an **item from the '50s**, what would you be?

If you were an **item from the '60s**, what would you be?

If you were an **item from the '70s**, what would you be?

If you were an **item from the '80s**, what would you be?

If you were an **item from the future**, what would you be?

**YOU MUST CHOOSE!**

If you were a **breakfast**, what would you be?

If you were a **politician**, who would you be?

If you were a **soup**, what would you be?

If you were a **shampoo**, what would you be?

Did you know?

> *Researchers are working on Pert Minus, which is not quite a shampoo, not quite a conditioner.\**

\*Factuality exaggerated.

**YOU MUST CHOOSE!**

# Which of these **Rorschach inkblots** represents you?

**YOU MUST CHOOSE!**

151

Are you...

**Tea** or **coffee?**

**Madonna** or **whore?**

**Hunter** or **prey?**

**Apple** or **orange?**

**Stapler** or **beret?**

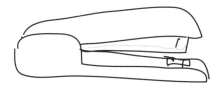

**YOU MUST CHOOSE!**

### If you were **one of the doodles in this book**,
what would you be?

### If you were a **Pixar character**, who would you be?

### If you were a **section in the Dewey Decimal system**
(the various book sections in the library), what would you be?

Things to consider: Is there anyone more overrated than Dewey of the Dewey Decimal system? This guy immortalized his name simply by saying "Let's put these books here and those books there." A guy should not become a part of common vocabulary for telling people where to put stuff. The same thing goes for Kelvin of temperature fame and Moh of Mohs's Hardness Scale. How hard is it to say talc is the softest and diamonds are the hardest? Big deal. Moh is worthless. Dewey is even less. Next caller.

**YOU MUST CHOOSE!**

## Which one of you...

Which of you or your friends is... **velvet**?

Which of you or your friends is... **Thor**?

Which of you or your friends is... a **crossword puzzle**? A **Sudoku**? A **word find**?

Which of you or your friends is... an **armadillo**?

Which couple that you know is... **Mentos and Diet Coke**?

If you were a **vaudeville act**, what would you be?

If you were a **prime time show**, what would you be?
Some to choose from: *24*, *The Office*, *So You Think You Can Dance*, *Deal or No Deal*

If your life were a **first date**, what would you be? Where?
How does it go? How far does it go?

If you were **bedroom clothing** or **lingerie**,
what would you be?

**YOU MUST CHOOSE!**

# The Death Page

If you were a **means of murder**, what would you be?

If you were a **death**, what would you be? (Act it out.)

If you were a **cemetery plot**, what would you be? Or are you ashes in an urn or tossed somewhere?

*Question of character:*

What do you want written on your gravestone? Some ideas: a map of the cemetery with a "You Are Here" marker; an eye doctor chart; "I'm with stupid" pointing to your spouse's plot.

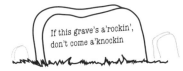

If this grave's a'rockin', don't come a'knockin

**YOU MUST CHOOSE!**

156

**If you were a bowel movement**, what would you be?

**If you were a cloud type**, what would you be?

**If you were a style of painting**, what would you be?

**If you were an island**, which would you be?
Things to consider: Would you be tropical? Cold? Civilized? Are you more of a peninsula? Maybe an archipelago or an isthmus?

**YOU MUST CHOOSE!**

157

If you were a **facial complexion**, what would you be?

If you were a **bowling round**, what would you be?
Score it, if you know how the hell to score bowling.

If you were a **skating move**, what would you be?

If you were a **pair of pants**, what would you be?
Some to choose from: a pair of pleated khaki slacks, jean shorts,
sweat pants

**YOU MUST CHOOSE!**

# You Are Something

If you were **something hung on a wall**, what would you be?

If you were **something in an office**, what would you be?

If you were **something in sight now**, from where you are, what would you be?

If you were **something in a wallet**, what would you be?

*Question of character:*

What is in your wallet right now?  Predict what is in other people's wallets.

**YOU MUST CHOOSE!**

# Be All That You Can Be

If you were a **military rank**, what would you be?

If you were a **war** or **battle**, what would you be?

If you were a **branch of the military**, which would you be?

If you were a **vehicle used in war**, what would you be?

*Question of character:*

Did you play war as a kid? What did you imagine? Did you pretend to play dead?

**YOU MUST CHOOSE!**

You are a **bookshelf**. Describe 5 titles on you.

If you were a **pet**, what would you be?

If you were a **crop**, what would you be?

If you were **lighting in a movie**, what would you be?

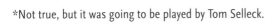

Did you know?

*The part of Indiana Jones was originally going to be played by Fran Tarkenton.*\*

\*Not true, but it was going to be played by Tom Selleck.

**YOU MUST CHOOSE!**

If you were a **Christmas gift**, what would you be?

If you were **something you'd find on the human body**, what would you be?

If you were **something that writes**, what would you be?

If you were a **line**—straight, curvy, crooked, whatever—what would you be? Draw it.

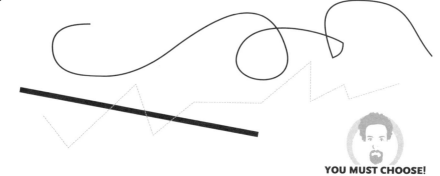

**YOU MUST CHOOSE!**

# Celebrities

Need some suggestions for the "I Am Thinking of a Celebrity" game?
We've provided a list below to get you started:

Dick Cheney
Britney Spears
Johnny Depp
Adolf Hitler
Bill O'Reilly
Dr. Phil
Mike Tyson
Peyton Manning
Diddy
Jesus Christ
Pamela Anderson
George Washington
George Washington Carver
George Washington Carver McGubbern
Larry David
Prince Charles
Al Gore

Brad Pitt
Robert DeNiro
Oprah Winfrey
Mike Tyson
Martha Stewart
Mr. T.
Will Ferrell
Roseanne Barr
Gandhi
Phil Bautista
Paris Hilton
The Rock
Elvis
Joe Piscopo
Anthony Hopkins
LeBron James
LeBron Gomberg

# Answer Page

## Answers

**Quiz 1: George Clooney**

**Quiz 2: Donald Trump**

**Quiz 3: George Bush**

**Quiz 4: Angelina Jolie**

# About The Authors

**Justin Heimberg** is a comedy writer who has written for all media including movies, TV, books, and magazines. He, along with David Gomberg, runs Falls Media, an entertainment company specializing in providing short and funny creative services and products.

**David Gomberg** is notably different from other oozes. Being a growth, he is fixed to one place and cannot move or attack. For the most part, he is forced to feed off of vegetable, organic or metallic substances in an underground wall. If he grows on a ceiling, however, he can sense if someone passes below, and drops onto them. Living creatures touched by Gomberg eventually turn into Gomberg themselves. Gomberg is vulnerable to light, heat, frost, and cure disease spells. Gomberg is mindless and cannot speak. As such, he is regarded as neutral in alignment. Gomberg will re-grow if even the tiniest residue remains, and can germinate to form a full sized ooze again years later.

# About the Deity

The ringmaster/MC/overlord of the *Would You Rather...* empire is "the Deity." Psychologically and physically a cross between Charles Manson and Gabe Kaplan, the Deity is the one responsible for creating and presenting the WWYB questions. It is the Deity who orders, without exception, that you must choose. No one knows exactly why he does this; suffice to say, it's for reasons beyond your understanding. The Deity communicates with you not through speech, nor telepathy, but rather through several sharp blows to the stomach that vary in power and location. Nearly omnipotent, often ruthless, and obsessed with former NBA seven-footers, the Deity is a random idea generator with a peculiar predilection for intervening in your life in the strangest ways.

# About "Would You Rather...?" Books:

Us guys, the authors of the *Would You Rather...?* books, believe that the great joys in life are the times spent hanging out with your friends, laughing. Our books aim to facilitate that. They are Socially Interactive Humor Books. SIHB's. Damnit, that acronym sucks! Let's try again... Socially Interactive Games & Humor SIGH... exactly the opposite of what we are looking for in an abbreviation. Son of a bitch. Alright look, these books make you think in interesting ways and talk to your friends, and laugh and be funny. They are, and they make you, imaginative and irreverent. Lots of bang for your buck (and vice versa.) *WYR* books provide 3-300 hrs of entertainment depending on how painfully retarded your reading pace is. So take these books, hang out with your friends, and have a good time.

# Other *Would You Rather...?*® Books:

*Would You Rather...?: Love & Sex* asks you to ponder such questions as:

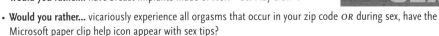

- **Would you rather...** orgasm once every ten years *OR* once every ten seconds?

- **Would you rather...** have to have sex in the same position every night *OR* have to have sex in a different position every night (you can never repeat)?

- **Would you rather...** have breast implants made of Nerf® *OR* Play-Doh®?

- **Would you rather...** vicariously experience all orgasms that occur in your zip code *OR* during sex, have the Microsoft paper clip help icon appear with sex tips?

*Would You Rather...?: Love & Sex* can be read alone or played together as a game.  Laugh-out-loud funny, uniquely imaginative, and deceptively thought-provoking, *Would You Rather...?: Love & Sex* is simultaneously the authors' most mature and immature work yet!

### *Would You Rather...? 2: Electric Boogaloo*

Another collection of over three hundred absurd alternatives and demented  dilemmas. Filled with wacky wit, irreverent humor and twisted pop-culture references.

### *Would You Rather...?: Pop Culture Edition*

A brand new collection of deranged dilemmas and preposterous predicaments, featuring celebrities and trends from popular culture.  Ponder and debate questions like: *Would you rather... be machine-gunned to death with Lite-Brite pegs or be assassinated by Cabbage Patch Dolls?*

### *Would You Rather...?: Illustrated*

Tired of having to visualize these dilemmas yourself? No need anymore with this book of masterfully illustrated *Would You Rather...?* dilemmas. Now you can see what it looks like to be attacked by hundreds of Pilsbury Doughboys, get hole-punched to death, sweat cheese, or have pubic hair that grows an inch every second. A feast for the eyes and imagination, *Would You Rather...?: Illustrated* gives Salvador Dali a run for his money.

### *Would You Rather...?'s What's Your Price?*

*Would you punch your grandmother in the stomach as hard as you can for $500,000?* There are no wrong answers but hundreds of "wrong" questions in an irresistibly irreverent book.

### *Would You Rather...? for Kids*

The first book in the series written and designed for kids ages 8 and older, *Would You Rather...? for Kids* features hundreds of devilish dilemmas and imaginative illustrations! Kids will crack up as they ponder questions such as: **Would you rather...** have a tape-dispensing mouth *OR* a bottle opening nostril?

# More Books by Falls Media

### The Official Movie Plot Generator

"A Coffee Table Masterpiece" - *Newsweek*.

*The Official Movie Plot Generator* is a unique and interactive humor book that offers 27,000 hilarious movie plot possibilities you create, spanning every genre of cinema from feel-good family fun to hard-boiled crime drama to soft-core pornography. Just flip the book's ninety tabs until you find a plot combination you like.

For movie fans or anyone who likes to laugh a lot with little effort, *The Official Movie Plot Generator* is a perfect gift and an irresistible, offbeat diversion.

### Pornification

"For every legit movie, there exists (at least theoretically), a porn version of that movie." *Pornification* includes over 500 "pornified" titles, along with hysterical quizzes, games and challenges. There's something for everyone, from *Cold Mountin'* to *The Fast and Bicurious* to *Malcolm XXX*, so open up and enjoy!

### *The Yo Momma Vocabulary Builder*

Increasing word power sounds like one of those dreary chores best pawned off on somebody else. *The Yo Momma Vocabulary Builder*, the first in Falls Media's series of irreverent, educational books, makes the activity not only endurable but irresistible. The authors use classic dissing and one-upsmanship to slyly introduce a wide range of words.

# Available at
# www.wouldyourather.com
# www.falls-media.com
# www.classlesseducation.com

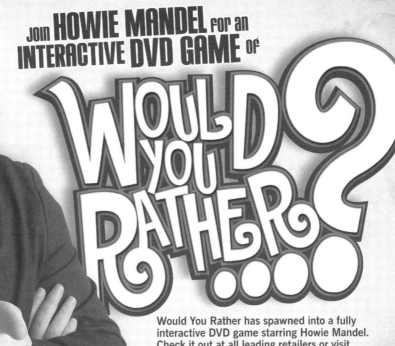

## Wrong End
## Do Not Open

Did you think this was a **Hebrew book**? Or are you **one of those people who flips to the last page of a book first**? Hey, it's ok, we do it too. Look, just do us a favor and turn to the front. We don't want to write the intro twice. And we don't know enough Hebrew.

*Shalom.*